This book was given to: Date:

Donnamarie Moynihan   _8-31-00_

Handed on to: Date:

_____   _____

_____   _____

_____   _____

_____   _____

_____   _____

The Whimsical Verse of

Olly-O™

The Whimsical Verse of

Olly-O™

by
Molly James

Featuring the Paper Sculpture of
Ron Chespak

To Donna Marie
Molly James
Happy Birthday!

Published by
Olly-O Enterprises, Inc.
Corona del Mar, CA 92625

Printed in the United States of America. Library of Congress Number: 98-91357 ISBN: 0-9662989-0-X

Contents

THE BUSY BUZZY BEE 4

THE CHATTY LION CAT 10

LOUIE THE LAZY LIZARD 16

THE PINK AND PURPLE FISH 22

THE OLD, OLD, OLD, OLD, OWL 28

SILVER FOX FRIENDLY 34

THE BUSY BUZZY BEE

I took a walk one windy day
To watch that teasing wind at play.

It swooped in gusts across the ground
To push the leaves and dust around

And whiffed through all the flower beds
To make the flowers bob their heads.

Then right beyond, three feet at best,
One flower bobbed more than the rest.

I went to see what I could see.
Inside, asleep, I saw a bee!

I guess I woke him though for he
Came wide awake and stared at me.

Then with a quick shake of his head
He stretched his wings and firmly said,

"I'm very busy, can't you see?
So if you please don't bother me.

There's quite a lot for me to do.
I simply cannot talk to you.

I hate to be discourteous
But buzzing is quite serious.

I'm not just cute and I'm not just fuzzy.
I'm very busy and very buzzy."

He flew a little ways away
Then thought of something else to say.

"One more thing," he said relanding,
"Try to be more understanding."

I tried to say I understood
But he went on before I could.

"Think just a minute now," he said,
"Who makes the honey for your bread?"

As I began to say, *"You do,"*
Away again he quickly flew.

Then, just as quickly he returned
Appearing very much concerned.

"Hard as I fly," he buzzed crossly,
"Something seems to push and toss me.

*When I start to buzz so busy
Something makes me feel quite dizzy."*

"Why it's the wind," I told poor bee.
"The wind?" he shouted angrily.

He shook a wing at me and cried,
"Just why was I not notified?

*You'll not find very many bees
At work today in all this breeze."*

Just then the wind whirled him around.
Kerplop, he landed on the ground.

"A *hurricane*," he cried. "A *gale!*
I've *been turned up head over tail.*"

The wind also had quite a knack
For getting bees up off their back.

It blew him round up on a leaf.
He stood there shivering with relief.

Then quietly from foot to wing
He stood not saying anything.

"*Are you all right?*" I asked him then.
He stood so still, I asked again.

He tried his wings, nodded slightly,
Said "*Good day,*" and bowed politely.

Flying off, he zigged and zagged some.
Wings were fine although they sagged some.

Then oh, so glad to be alive,
He made a bee line for his hive.

—Olly-O

9

THE CHATTY LION CAT

I took a walk one rainy day
   To where the baby monkeys play.

The trees and plants grew up so tall
   Just the giraffes could see them all.

The rain was falling fast and wet
   And got me wet as wet could get.

So I began to look about
   To find a place to wring me out.

Beneath a leaf as big as I
   I saw a spot that looked quite dry.

There even was a place to sit
So down I sat on top of it.

At once I heard a grouchy *"Ouch!"*
A grumbling lion was my couch.

And then he growled so terribly
He made me wish he was not he.

And everything from ground to sky
Shook, quaked and trembled, so did I.

His mouth was open very wide
As if to say, *"Please jump inside."*

11

I dared not move or turn my back
For fear I'd be his morning snack.

"I must be leaving soon," I said.
"You've really been a lovely bed.

I'll rest a minute from my walk.
Let's you and me just sit and talk

And laugh and kid and sing a song
Before I have to run along.

How's things? What's new? Have you been well?
I hope the family's feeling swell.

To talk," I sighed, "is quite a strain
When sitting on a lion's mane."

"Growl," he said, "*I'm tough and strong.*
You won't be sitting there for long."

I said to him, "*I must agree,*
     You're tough and strong but woe is me.

       You're really the least chatty cat
     Upon whose back I've ever sat."

He growled again and said, "*I'm King.*
I'm not the least of anything.

Before I eat you, you will see
How very chatty I can be.

Quick. Tell me how. In nothing flat
I'll be the greatest chatty cat."

I said to him, "*That would be grand,*"
     To teach him how, I'll have to stand.

       "*First close your eyes. That's the best way*
       To think of many things to say.

14

Now, *to be chatty, talk and talk,"*
And while he does I'll have a walk.

And as I quickly walked away
I could hear dear lion say,

"Two times two is forty four
If I had nine I'd ask for more.

The world is round, it isn't flat,
And I am the most chatty cat."

—Olly-O

LOUIE THE LAZY LIZARD

I took a walk one bright hot day
To where the desert turtles play.

The coarse dry earth baked by the heat
Crunched and scrunched beneath my feet.

The scattered rocks were smooth and bare.
Some sagebrush grew up here and there.

I found one rock where I could sit
And look about and rest a bit.

There on a rock right next to me
A lizard stretched quite peacefully.

Without a move from tail to head
He cleared his throat and slowly said,

"I'm Louie the Lazy Lizard as lazy as can be.
While you take forty winks
I'll take nine hundred ninety three.

I know the least about the most
That fact you need not doubt.
My waking time's spent thinking of
What not to think about.

I eat if something happens by and drink if raindrops fall.
I have no door or doorbell so no one can come to call.

I do not have a telephone to answer when it rings.
I do not have a mailbox so no mail the mailman brings.

I have no books or radio and I have no TV.
I have no job, no place to go, my time's completely free.

I simply lie upon this rock and bask here in the sun.
Now that I think about it, I'm not having any fun!"

He raised his head, looked to the sky,
Puffed up his chest and blinked an eye.

"The first thing that I'll do," he said *"is run at least a mile.*
I'll grow so strong that all will think that I'm a crocodile.

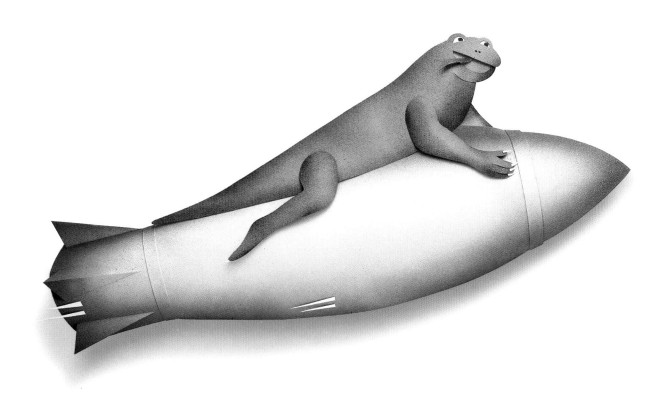

I'll write ten thousand letters and get a mailbox too,
And buy a dozen newspapers to find out what is new.

I'll get a job and work real hard
And then next thing you know,
I'll have a telephone that rings
And then a radio.

I'll make a million friends at least
And have them all to tea,
To hear them tell about themselves
And how much they like me.

I'll wisely spend my money, then
With what I haven't spent
I'll take a plane to Washington
And run for president."

He flipped his tail and sped away
And through the dust I heard him say,

"Good bye my friend. So glad you came.
I'll be back just as soon
As I have finished being
The first lizard on the moon."

—Olly-O

THE PINK AND PURPLE FISH

I took a walk one sunny day
To where the small sandpipers play.

I watched the ocean touch its toes
And felt salt spray upon my nose.

I saw the sea gulls soar with ease
By catching rides on every breeze.

A spider crab went scurrying,
Away from me went hurrying.

I wouldn't want to tell him so,
But I was glad to see him go.

And then I listened carefully
For I heard something in that sea.

I heard a swoosh and saw a swish.
Up popped a pink and purple fish.

"Hello," I said and waved my hand.
With that he swam right up on land.

Then with a twist stood on his head
And from that strange position said,

"We fish you know can't sing a note
Though we have lots of scales.
We cannot tell a story well
Although we do have tails.

We've never learned to read or write
Though we have lots of schools.
But we could build a people pole
If we just had the tools.

Sea horses swim around us but never wear a saddle
And I've never seen a swordfish carried off to battle.

The fiddler crabs can't play a note.
I know they don't know how.
I've much more I could tell you
But that's quite enough for now."

He flopped himself back in the sea
Then called back to me wistfully,

"Oh my you are a lucky one.
Oh how, oh how, I wish
That I could hear the wisdom of
A pink and purple fish."

I think a tear dropped from my eye.
    I did not like to say good bye.

        Next time I walk again that way
        I'll find that spot and then I'll say,

"Dear waves and breakers hear my wish.
Please send the pink and purple fish."

—Olly-O

THE OLD, OLD, OLD, OLD, OWL

I took a walk one chilly night.
In coat and cap I bundled tight.

With chattering teeth and shivering knees
I found a path through pepper trees.

And then by walking oh so fast
I finally got me warm at last.

So I slowed down and looked around
At shadows dancing on the ground.

The things I hear and see at night
Are scarier than when it's light.

So I jumped quick behind a tree
When I heard something speak to me.

"Well, well, who's this?"
 The something said.

"Why aren't you home tucked in your bed
With covers up about your head?"

I peeked around the tree and sighed.
Oh silly, silly me to hide.

It was the old, old owl I'd heard.
"Hello," said I. "Hello, wise bird."

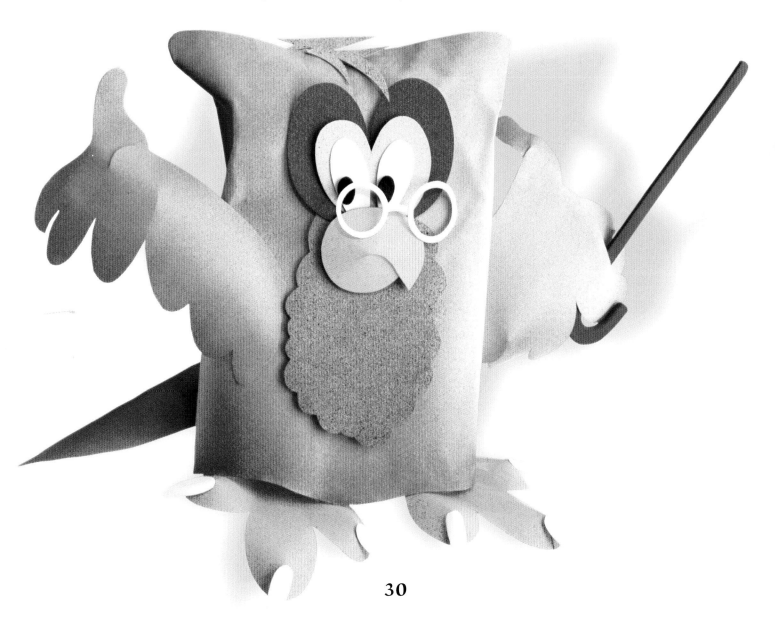

30

He blinked three blinks then cocked his head.
He thought and thought and then he said,

"And I suppose that you've been told
That I am old, old, old, old, old?"

I shook my head quite eagerly
And wondered, how old can he be?

"I guess," he said, "that all in all
I've lived as long as I recall.

Too busy I am much, much, much
To give a thought to such, such, such."

We laughed and he went on to say
He worked all night and slept all day.

He told me that his time was spent
In thinking of things to invent.

"Such as," he said, "I'll name a few
Of all the things I have to do.

Now there's a rooster who's too slow
To wake each day in time to crow
Before the sun begins to glow.

I must make him a clock to check.
A little one that weighs a speck.
One he can wear around his neck.

And for a duck who's getting old
But likes the water, so I'm told
    Except he's always catching cold

    I'm working on a lovely pair
        Of rubber boots
            for him to wear
            To wade about in
            here and there.

He stopped and smiled a little while
And then a laugh grew from the smile.

He laughed until two tears were shed
Before he stopped and then he said,

"Poor pig told me with quivering chin,
Her tail is straight and rather thin.
I must make her a piggy pin

To hold her tail up in a curl
Just tight enough to not unfurl
So she can be a glamour girl."

He paused then said, *"Friend Olly-O*
How late it is. Now you must go."

We said good night. I walked away.
I wished my night could be my day.

—Olly-O

SILVER FOX FRIENDLY

I took a walk one wintry day
To where the fawns and foxes play.

I gathered soft handfuls of snow
To make round snowballs I could throw.

The forest was so white and still
Without a single sound until

Something made an awful racket,
Something in a silver jacket.

And through the snow capped brush and rocks
There tumbled out a laughing fox.

He rolled about and laughed with glee
And turned a handspring merrily.

Each time he looked at me some more
His laugh grew louder than before.

So I could very clearly see
The thing that he laughed at was me.

And after romping all about
He sat down panting, all tired out.

"*My friend,*" he grinned, "*you are a sight.*
It's fun to watch you walk upright.

And as your friend, I must advise
You're in a very poor disguise.

Why I would know you any place.
I never do forget a face.

Now let me think. Where did we meet?
Would you mind walking on four feet?"

I said, "I can't do what you say
For I was born to walk this way."

He paused and then with paw to brow
He gaily said, "I know you now!

My friends the birds walk as you do.
Are you by chance a cockatoo?"

When I said "No" he jumped aside
And rushed behind a bush to hide.

Then he knew that he was seeing
A two footed human being.

"You're small," he said, "make no mistake,
But I've a quick fast trip to make.

Right away I must begin it.
You might grow up any minute."

He twirled to run but spun around
And skidded backward on the ground.

He landed at my feet and said,
"Well, I won't run, I'll walk instead."

He rose to walk but he had put
His bushy tail beneath his foot.

He tripped and slipped and bumped and bounced,
Then sat by me as he announced,

*"I have decided to intend
To make you my first human friend."*

We laughed and talked about the snow
And of the things sly foxes know.

And when we said good-bye at last,
He waved and called, *"Don't grow too fast!"*

—Olly-O

Olly-O
Contributors

Written & Narrated by
Molly James

Featuring the Paper Sculpture of
Ron Chespak

Original Music Composed
& Directed by
Hoyt Curtin

Recorded at
RCA Studios

Photography by
Michael Jarrett

Production Art by
Keven Ellison

Lithography by
Orange Ink

Pre-press by
Doug Robertson, Design Café

Delivery Accommodations by
Jeff Bisnett

Web Site by
BleuBoy Chicago

Trademarks and Copyrights by
**Carlo F. Van den Bosch, Esquire
Sheppard, Mullin, Richter
& Hampton LLP**

Printed in U.S.A.